A FOCUS ON...

MARRIAGE & EQUALITY

By John Wood

BookLife
PUBLISHING

©2018
BookLife Publishing
King's Lynn
Norfolk PE30 4LS

A catalogue record for this
book is available from the
British Library.

ISBN: 978-1-78637-376-2

Written by:
John Wood

Edited by:
Kirsty Holmes

Designed by:
Dan Scase

CONTENTS

Words that look like **this** are explained in the glossary on **PAGE 31.**

MARRIAGE

Many adults are in romantic **relationships**. When two people are in a romantic relationship, they are called a couple. Couples are **affectionate** to each other; they often live together and they might have children. Marriage is a celebration of the couple's love, and an agreement that they will look after each other and share their lives together. This agreement is recorded by the government.

IMPORTANCE IN RELIGION

The idea of marriage is very old. Marriage may have become popular because it helped create a strong family where the children were looked after. Even though marriage wasn't invented by religion, it is seen as a very important thing in religions all around the world. For example: in Christianity, marriage is a gift from God, and it is part of God's plan that two people should live together as a married couple.

FACT

THE PROPHET MUHAMMAD, WHO IS THE founder OF ISLAM, SAID THAT 'MARRIAGE IS HALF OF RELIGION', MEANING THAT IT IS VERY IMPORTANT.

GOVERNMENT AND THE LAW

Married couples are sometimes treated differently to unmarried couples. Taxes, for example, are when a government takes a bit of money from everyone and uses it to run the country. In many countries, married couples might pay less tax than unmarried couples. People who are married can also share their money and belongings with each other more easily, especially when it comes to passing on their belongings or wealth after they die. This is called inheritance, and it is much easier to do between people who are married.

MARRIED COUPLES MIGHT ALSO FIND IT EASIER TO ADOPT CHILDREN.

MARRIAGE CERTIFICATES

Depending on what country people get married in, there are different **documents** that people need to sign. This is often called a marriage certificate. A copy of the certificate is kept by the married couple and the government as a record of the marriage. Once the couple has signed the marriage certificate, their marriage will be legally recognised by the government.

A MARRIAGE CERTIFICATE

WEDDINGS AND RELIGION

Most people celebrate their marriage with a ceremony, called a wedding. In history, weddings have been a religious celebration, and many weddings still have religious parts today. However, there are many different religions and each has different wedding **traditions**. These wedding traditions are often very old, and include special songs, clothes, food, speeches and prayers. Before or during a wedding, the couple will sign the marriage certificate, and afterwards there is often a big celebration, called a reception.

CHURCH

MOSQUE

PLACES OF WORSHIP

Religious weddings are often held in a place of worship. Jewish weddings often take place in or outside a synagogue, while Sikh weddings may be inside a temple. Christian weddings are held in churches, so God can witness the marriage. However, not all religious weddings take place at a special building. Islamic weddings may take place in a mosque, but they can also take place at someone's house, or at a town hall. A Hindu wedding is often held at the bride's house. A special altar is made, called the mandap.

SIKH TEMPLE

MANDAP

SYNAGOGUE

OFFICIANT

An officiant is a person who performs the wedding. In a religious wedding, the officiant is a type of religious leader who has the power to perform religious duties. These leaders are called the clergy, and they have different names in different religions. In a Christian wedding, this person will be a priest or a vicar. In Sikhism, an Amritdhari Sikh performs the marriage ceremony.

RABBI

IN A JEWISH WEDDING, A RABBI USUALLY OVERSEES THE CEREMONY.

VOWS

Another important part of a religious ceremony are the vows and prayers. Vows are the promises that the married couple make to each other in front of their god or the people who are at the wedding. Some religions, like Christianity, have a strict set of vows that are **recited** at weddings. These vows are about the rules, ideas and traditions that are important to that religion. In some religions, like Islam, there are usually no vows. Instead, the imam, or other officiant, will tell the couple their duties within the marriage, and also recite prayers or readings.

FACT

THERE IS NO OFFICIAL CLERGY IN ISLAM. HOWEVER, IMAMS, WHO ARE RELIGIOUS LEADERS THAT LEAD PRAYERS, SOMETIMES WED COUPLES TOGETHER.

SOMETIMES COUPLES WILL WRITE THEIR OWN PERSONAL VOWS WHICH ARE SAID ALONGSIDE THE TRADITIONAL RELIGIOUS VOWS.

NON-RELIGIOUS MARRIAGE

REGISTRARS ARE LICENSED BY THE GOVERNMENT TO CARRY OUT WEDDINGS.

CIVIL MARRIAGE

Atheists are people who do not believe in any god, so they might want a non-religious wedding. A non-religious wedding is called a civil wedding. At a civil wedding, the officiant is usually a **registrar**, or sometimes a mayor. There are no places of worship used in a civil wedding; the marriage usually takes place in a building which has been approved by the government. This might be a hotel, a hall, or even somebody's house. Civil weddings are usually celebrated with a reception or party too, and can be very personal to the couple.

HUMANIST MARRIAGE

Humanists are people who believe that humans give meaning and importance to their own lives, and do not worship a god. Humanists have civil marriages, with humanist celebrations and ceremonies. A humanist wedding is very personal. The married couple will usually write their own vows, and will decide on their own traditions, food and clothing. Instead of religious prayers, the couple often reads from books or poems which are important to them, or to humanist ideas. Each humanist wedding is very unique because there are no strict rules when it comes to traditions.

CIVIL PARTNERSHIPS

A civil partnership is not a marriage, but in many ways it is very similar. Couples who have a civil partnership sign documents to make their romantic relationship official, and this is recorded by the government. Civil partners have similar **rights** and duties to married couples. There is no religious ceremony or wedding in a civil partnership, but the couple may choose to celebrate their partnership with a reception afterwards.

FIND OUT MORE ABOUT SAME-SEX MARRIAGE ON PAGE 28.

FACT

IN THE UK, AROUND 72% OF MARRIAGES HAVE NON-RELIGIOUS CEREMONIES.

CIVIL PARTNERSHIPS AND SOME CIVIL MARRIAGES TAKE PLACE IN A REGISTRY OFFICE, LIKE THIS ONE.

In many countries, civil partnerships are only for same-sex couples, although this may soon change. In countries where same-sex couples are not allowed to get married, they may have the option to have a civil partnership instead. People might want to have a civil partnership because they are not religious, and do not want to be involved with any religious ceremonies. They might not like the traditions of marriage, or disagree with what marriage stands for. Many people believe that both options should be available to every couple.

MARRIAGE TRADITIONS AROUND THE WORLD

At a Jewish wedding, it is tradition to wrap a piece of glass in a cloth and then stamp on it. The glass shatters, and everyone shouts 'Mazel Tov!' which means congratulations or good luck. This tradition reminds everyone of the suffering that the Jewish people have gone through, and shows that there is always darkness in the world, even in times of celebration.

At a Hindu wedding, the couple lights a **sacred** fire. Offerings are made to the fire and prayers are said. The couple then walk around the fire and recite vows and promises to each other.

At a Christian wedding, there is usually a wedding cake at the reception. It is tradition for the married couple to cut the cake together.

In Bermuda, the married couple are given a cake with a **sapling** on top. The married couple plant the sapling in the garden of their new house. In this tradition, the growing sapling **represents** the growing love of the couple as they get older.

Families are kept separate during the Christian and Jewish wedding ceremonies, with each family sitting on a different side of the **aisle**. In Jewish weddings, the couple walks down the aisle together with both of their parents. In Christian weddings, the groom walks down first and the bride follows later, usually accompanied by her father.

Traditional wedding clothing can be very different around the world. In Hindu weddings, the married couple and guests wear bright, vibrant colours and lots of jewellery. A Hindu bride's outfit is made up of 16 different pieces.

In traditional Cuban weddings, the couple and guests take part in the 'baile del dollar', which means dollar dance. While the married couple are dancing, people might interrupt to dance with either the bride or the groom. The person will then pin money to the bride and groom's clothes, or put the money in a box or bag.

FACT

HINDU WEDDINGS LAST FOR THREE DAYS.

11

EQUALITY

BEING DIFFERENT

Someone's identity is all the things that make them who they are. Identity is made up of lots of things, such as where a person is from, what they like and dislike, how old they are, what religion they follow, or whether they are a boy or a girl. Having a different identity is a good thing, but it often leads to people being treated differently.

Sometimes it is fair to treat people differently – for example, a child should not be expected to do adult things. However, many times it can be unfair to treat people differently. For example, girls and boys should be able to play the same games at school if they want to. It would be unfair if they were forced to play a certain game because of their identity.

THE IMPORTANCE OF EQUALITY

Equality is the idea of treating people fairly or the same, so everybody has equal rights and **opportunities**. Although people can be very different, it is important that they are all treated equally. Equality gives everyone a fair chance to live how they want to live. People who are equal are free because they are not being stopped from doing anything because of their differences.

PEOPLE SHOULD BE ABLE TO CELEBRATE THEIR DIFFERENCES.

EQUALITY AND INEQUALITY

Inequality is the opposite of equality – it means people are not treated equally, and do not have the same rights and opportunities. History is full of examples of people being treated unfairly because of parts of their identity. Racism is a type of behaviour where people do and say things that are unfair, upsetting or **violent** against people who have a different colour of skin. Racism is wrong, and is extremely unfair and hurtful.

TREATING WOMEN UNFAIRLY BECAUSE THEY ARE WOMEN IS CALLED SEXISM. MANY PEOPLE GO TO **protests** TO FIGHT AGAINST SEXISM.

EQUALITY IN MARRIAGE

In a marriage, both people should have the same rights and opportunities as each other. Both people should be treated the same in the law, and nobody should be forced to do anything that they don't want to do. For example, in an equal marriage both people should be able to go to work if they want to. Nobody should be forced to stay at home and look after the house. Jobs and chores around the house should also be shared equally.

FACT

THROUGHOUT THE 20TH CENTURY, THE CIVIL RIGHTS MOVEMENT IN AMERICA TACKLED RACISM AND AIMED TO ACHIEVE EQUALITY FOR BLACK AMERICANS. THE MOVEMENT PUT AN END TO MANY LAWS THAT WERE UNFAIR TO BLACK PEOPLE.

MARRIAGE EQUALITY THROUGHOUT HISTORY

KINGS AND QUEENS

Marriage used to be a way of strengthening relationships between groups of people. In 5th century England, Anglo-Saxons would use marriage to bring different tribes together, so families could work with each other and trade more. This used to be the case for royal families too. The king would decide who the prince or princess would marry. Often, the king would choose a royal family member from another country who the king wanted to make friends with.

Nobody could argue with the king's choice, especially not princesses. They were expected to get married, no matter how they felt about the person they were getting married to. This was very unequal, as people did not have the choice of who they were to marry, especially if they were a woman.

DOWRIES

A dowry is a gift or a payment made by the wife's family and given to the husband's family. Dowries were popular in parts of the world such as Europe, Africa and India. However, dowries can lead to inequality in marriage for women. Arguments over dowries have led to violence against women, especially if the wife's family cannot find enough money.

DOWRIES STILL EXIST IN SOME PARTS OF THE WORLD, LIKE INDIA, EVEN THOUGH IT IS AGAINST THE LAW.

THE MARRIED WOMAN'S PROPERTY ACT

In 1848 in the US, and 1870 in the UK, the Married Woman's Property Act was passed. This law meant that women would be treated equally to men in owning **property**, earning money and collecting inheritance. In many countries before this act, a married woman's property, money and **possessions** were usually controlled by her husband. For many years, women were thought to belong to their husband, as if they were his property. However, this act was an important step in creating equality for women in marriage. Anything that a woman earned after this act belonged to her, and not her husband.

THIS IS A WEDDING PHOTO FROM AROUND 1860, AS THE MARRIED WOMAN'S PROPERTY ACT WAS BEING PASSED.

EQUAL CREDIT OPPORTUNITY ACT

There are even examples of marriage inequality in more recent times. Throughout most of the 20th century, women couldn't get a **credit card** on their own, but men could. In 1974, the US passed a law called the Equal Credit Opportunity Act. This allowed women to apply for credit cards or the ability to borrow money from a bank without needing their husband's permission.

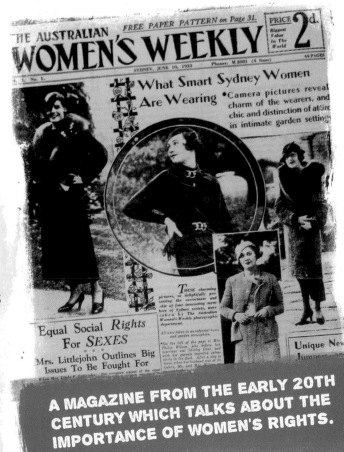

A MAGAZINE FROM THE EARLY 20TH CENTURY WHICH TALKS ABOUT THE IMPORTANCE OF WOMEN'S RIGHTS.

MARRIAGE EQUALITY TODAY

Today, marriage is a lot more equal in most parts of the world. In most countries, women and men are allowed to choose the partners that they want to marry, and dowries are often illegal now. It is also illegal in almost all countries to force someone to marry if they don't want to. Many **old-fashioned** ideas about marriage are changing too. For a long time, people thought that men should go to work while women look after the home. However, it is now accepted that women have a right to work, and that it is OK for men to stay at home and look after the house.

More and more countries are also passing laws so that anyone can marry each other, whether this is a man and a woman, two men or two women. This makes it more equal for people who want to be in a same-sex marriage. However, while most people agree that both people in a marriage should be treated the same, marriage equality does not exist all over the world yet. There are still some old-fashioned traditions and ideas that haven't changed.

OLD TRADITIONS

Many people think that some old traditions in marriage don't represent what **society** is actually like anymore. Because of this, many people think that some parts of marriage should be changed.

MARRIAGE CERTIFICATE

CERTIFIED COPY OF AN ENTRY OF MARRIAGE   GIVEN AT THE GENERAL REGISTER OFFICE

SAMPLE CERTIFICATE

For example, in the UK, the fathers of the couple getting married must sign the marriage certificate, but not the mothers. This is because the law was different a long time ago, and the father's permission was needed for a couple to marry. However, this is no longer the case. It is also the tradition in a Christian wedding for a father to walk his daughter down the aisle and give her away to the groom. In history, daughters were seen as the property of their father, and he could choose who she married. However, this is also no longer true, and the only reason this still happens at weddings is because the tradition is old. Many people do not want to take part in these traditions because it represents inequality in marriage.

THIS FATHER IS GIVING AWAY HIS DAUGHTER AT HER WEDDING.

FORCED MARRIAGE

In a forced marriage, one or both people do not want to get married. In some cases, people are physically or emotionally harmed until they agree to get married. Sometimes people are blackmailed into getting married. Being blackmailed is when someone threatens to do something that will be bad if you don't do what they say. Forced marriages are more common for women and girls; in 85% of forced marriages, women and girls were the victims, which shows the inequality that still exists in marriage today. It can be very hard to know just how many forced marriages there are because most of them are covered up and not talked about.

WHY DOES FORCED MARRIAGE HAPPEN?

Sometimes people are forced to marry because of **honour**. A family might have promised that their child would marry someone when they are grown up. Because they don't want to go back on that promise, the family might force their child into marriage.

SOME FAMILIES FORCE THEIR CHILD TO MARRY SO THAT THE FAMILY WEALTH IS SHARED WITH SOMEONE THAT THEY LIKE.

CHILD MARRIAGE

Marriage is for adults, but sometimes children are forced into marriage, even though it is illegal in most countries. In a child marriage, one or both of the people are under 18. In some cases, children that are 11 years old or younger are forced to marry. This is more common for women and girls, and they are often married to an adult.

CHILD MARRIAGE IS VERY DAMAGING BECAUSE IT STOPS EDUCATION AND OFTEN LEADS TO THE CHILD BEING CONTROLLED BY THEIR HUSBAND FOR THE REST OF THEIR LIVES.

WHY DOES CHILD MARRIAGE HAPPEN?

Child marriages often happen where there is also **gender inequality**. This usually means that girls are not **valued** and respected as much as boys, and society thinks it doesn't matter if they want to get married or not. A lot of the time, child marriage happens just because it is an old tradition in that country, and people think it is normal, even though it is not normal at all.

FACT ....
ALMOST A THIRD OF CHILD BRIDES ARE MARRIED TO MEN WHO ARE 21 OR OLDER.

THE FIGHT AGAINST CHILD MARRIAGE

The United Nations (UN) is an **international** organisation which tries to deal with problems in the world. In 2016, the UN announced that they would be putting their efforts into ending child marriage by 2030. This would protect millions of children around the world.

CHILD MARRIAGE ALSO OCCURS BECAUSE OF POVERTY. IF THE FAMILY CANNOT LOOK AFTER THEIR CHILD, THEY MIGHT FORCE THEM TO MARRY INTO A FAMILY THAT CAN.

THE UN FLAG

ARRANGED MARRIAGE

An arranged marriage is where a **matchmaker**, often the parents, finds the right husband or wife for someone. This is not the same as a forced marriage; both the husband and the wife need to agree to the arranged marriage. People who have arranged marriages think that their parents or matchmaker will have a better idea of who will be the best husband or wife.

JAPAN

Japan has a history of arranged marriages. Although they were less popular in the 1800s and 1900s, nowadays many people are having arranged marriages again. In Japan there are now 'omiai' agencies, which are companies that choose a marriage partner. Japanese people sometimes feel a lot of pressure to get married, which can be difficult when they lead busy lives going to work in big cities. Arranged marriages can be a safer and easier way to find a marriage partner. First, the couple will meet to see if they get along, and if they both say yes then the marriage is arranged.

JAPANESE MARRIAGE

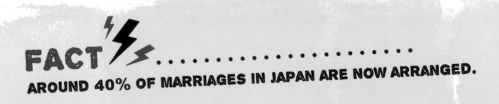

FACT
AROUND 40% OF MARRIAGES IN JAPAN ARE NOW ARRANGED.

INDIA

Arranged marriages are most common in South Asia, in countries like India and Pakistan. Families in India tend to be bigger, and are important in all parts of people's lives, including marriage. It is important that the family approve of a married partner in countries like India.

In some cultures, the husband and wife do not even see each other before the wedding. Most of the time, the couple only meet once before the marriage. In this meeting, they are joined by their parents, and the couple are never alone. Some people do not like the idea of an arranged marriage because they think it takes away the freedom to choose a partner. However, many people from India prefer an arranged marriage because they want help when picking a partner and organising the wedding. They also like the idea that both people are **committed** to each other straight away, and they don't have to worry about the other one leaving.

POLYGAMY

JACOB ZUMA

Polygamy (say: pol-ig-a-me) is when a person is married to more than one person. This usually means a man who has more than one wife. This might mean two wives, or it might mean many more than that. Jacob Zuma, South Africa's former president, had nine wives. Polygamy is more popular in some parts of the world than others. Around 47% of marriages in West Africa involved men having more than one wife. In countries like Libya, Iran and Egypt, polygamy is still legal. It is thought that polygamy was more common long ago in history, and the reason it is still popular in some places is because it is a tradition.

THIS MAP SHOWS WHERE POLYGAMY IS LEGAL. THE COUNTRIES THAT ARE COLOURED IN BLACK STILL ALLOW POLYGAMY.

AMERICAN STATES HAVE TRIED TO PUT A STOP TO POLYGAMY BY PASSING LAWS THAT MAKE IT ILLEGAL.

Polygamy sometimes happens in the US too but it isn't shown on the map because it isn't very common and it's against the law. There are a group of Christians called Mormons who used to allow polygamy and many of them live in the US. However, when Mormons decided to stop polygamy, some people created their own religious groups and called themselves 'fundamentalist Mormons'. Unlike most other Mormons, these groups still have men who have many wives.

POLYGAMY AND INEQUALITY

Polygamy is often unfair and unequal because it is much more common for men to have more than one wife than it is for wives to have more than one husband. In a survey of more than 1,000 societies around the world, the University of Wisconsin found that only four of those societies allowed women to marry more than one man.

In an equal society, both men and women would be able to marry the same number of people. Polygamy can also lead to jealously between co-wives or co-husbands if some are treated differently to others. Polygamy can also create problems for unmarried women. Because some men are wealthy and have many wives, it means there are fewer women for others to marry. This means that unmarried women become very valuable, and are controlled by their families and forced to marry richer people who they might not want to marry. If there are not enough women for all the men, young girls may also be forced to marry, even if they are too young.

BIGAMY IS WHEN SOMEONE HAS MULTIPLE HUSBANDS OR WIVES BUT THEIR PARTNERS DON'T KNOW ABOUT EACH OTHER. THIS IS DIFFERENT TO POLYGAMY AND IS AGAINST THE LAW IN MANY COUNTRIES.

23

DIVORCE

If a couple is unhappy with their marriage and cannot solve their problems, they might not want to be married anymore. To end the marriage, the couple must get a divorce. A divorce is a way to legally end a marriage. The married couple have to sign lots of documents and send them to **court**. Even though divorce can be upsetting for the married couple and their family, it is important that people have the freedom to end a marriage if they want to.

CHILDREN AND DIVORCE

When a married couple get divorced, they will not want to live together anymore. If the married couple have children, this often means that the children will live with one parent for most of the time and see their other parent maybe at the weekends. This decision is different for every divorce, and the divorced couple might have to go to court to decide what will happen.

A COURTROOM

RELIGION

Divorce is seen as a bad thing in many religions because marriage is such an important and often sacred thing. Many religions such as Christianity, Hinduism and Islam only let couples divorce for special reasons – usually if one of the promises of marriage has been broken, such as one of the couples having a relationship with someone else.

COUPLES IN A RELIGIOUS MARRIAGE ARE TOLD TO TRY AND STAY TOGETHER BEFORE THEY THINK ABOUT GETTING A DIVORCE.

DIVORCE AND INEQUALITY

In the UK, divorce used to be illegal and people were forced to stay together even if they were unhappy. People could only get divorced after a law called the Matrimonial Causes Act was passed in 1857. However, even after 1857, it was much harder for women to divorce their husbands than it was for men to divorce their wives. Although marriage is much fairer today, women are still sometimes treated unfairly in divorce, especially if the couple have children. When a couple gets married and has children, one of them might decide to give up their job to look after the children. It has been more common for women to do this than men. This can stop women from having good, well-paying careers. After a divorce, this can mean that women find it hard to support themselves and their children.

THE FUTURE OF MARRIAGE

AROUND 11 MILLION PEOPLE GOT MARRIED IN CHINA IN 2016. HOWEVER THIS WAS 800,000 LESS THAN IN 2015.

NUMBER OF DIVORCES

The number of divorces every year is difficult to measure. However, information about divorce shows that the number of divorces is going up every year in many countries. In 2016, China's Ministry of Civil Affairs announced that there were more and more divorces every year. In the US, there are around 3.2 divorces per 1,000 people. In Europe, there are around 1.9 divorces per 1,000 people.

TRENDS

By looking at information about the number of marriages and divorces that people are getting, it is possible to imagine how marriage will change in the future. Information on marriage shows that fewer people are getting married nowadays. In England and Wales, there were 470,000 marriages in 1940, but only 231,000 in 2009. Each year, the number of marriages usually goes down. This trend is happening all over the world, including China, Japan and the United States.

ATHEISM VS RELIGION

Some people would say there are fewer marriages because marriage is becoming less important in today's world. This is partly because religion is also becoming less important in many societies. In western countries especially, there are more atheists and humanists, and fewer religious people. More and more people do not want to follow a god or the traditions of religion, including marriage.

RICHARD DAWKINS

RICHARD DAWKINS IS A FAMOUS ATHEIST. HE WRITES BOOKS AND GIVES SPEECHES ABOUT HIS BELIEF THAT THERE IS NO GOD.

GENDER EQUALITY

A rise in gender equality might also be a reason for a fall in marriage. Women all over the world rightfully realise that they are valuable and deserve to be treated the same as men. This leads to more divorce and fewer marriages because women do not need to be married to a man who will support them. Some people think that marriage is old-fashioned, and that it doesn't represent today's society.

WOMEN'S MARCHES SUCH AS THIS ONE ARE HELD ALL OVER THE WORLD TO SUPPORT GENDER EQUALITY.

SAME-SEX MARRIAGE

Same-sex marriage is a marriage between two people of the same sex, for example a marriage between two men or a marriage between two women. People who form relationships with people of the same sex are called gay or homosexual. In an equal and fair society, people who are homosexual should have the same access to marriage as other people.

HOMOPHOBIA

Homophobia is a word used when people are treated unfairly or hurt because they are homosexual. This includes hurting people with words or with violence. Homophobia has been widespread for a very long time, at least since the **Middle Ages** when people were more religious. Many very old religions, including Christianity and Islam, teach that homosexuality is wrong but not all Christians and Muslims believe this.

THESE PEOPLE ARE PROTESTING AGAINST HOMOPHOBIA.

THE RAINBOW FLAG IS A SYMBOL FOR GAY RIGHTS.

Even being homosexual was illegal in most countries in the early 20th century. For example, it wasn't until 1967 that it became legal in the UK. In countries such as Libya, Egypt, Iran and Saudi Arabia, homosexuality is still illegal. Until recently, same-sex marriage wasn't allowed in any country and a civil partnership was the only option, if the relationships were allowed to be recognised at all.

IMPORTANT EVENTS IN THE FIGHT FOR SAME-SEX MARRIAGE

- **1924:** The first gay rights group is set up. It is called the Society for Human Rights and it is based in Chicago, in the US.

- **1969:** In New York, police raided a pub called the Stonewall Inn, which was a popular place among gay people. This sparked protests for several days as gay people fought back against the police. Some people say that this started the gay civil rights movement in America.

- **1972:** The first pride march took place in London, with 2,000 people involved. Pride marches are demonstrations around the world that draw attention to the inequality that gay people face every day.

The Netherlands became the first country to legalise same-sex marriage in 2001. In 2015, the Supreme Court of the United States of America made same-sex marriage legal all over the US. More and more countries are making gay marriage legal, such as Canada and Spain in 2005, France and the UK in 2013, and Germany and Australia in 2017.

THE FIRST GAY MARRIAGE IN WASHINGTON STATE, UNITED STATES OF AMERICA

FIND OUT MORE

FIND OUT MORE ABOUT RELIGION AND MARRIAGE:

HINDUISM:
www.bbc.co.uk/schools/gcsebitesize/rs/
relationships/himarriageanddivorcerev1.shtml

CHRISTIANITY:
www.bbc.co.uk/schools/gcsebitesize/rs/
relationships/chmarriageanddivorcerev1.shtml

ISLAM:
www.bbc.co.uk/schools/gcsebitesize/rs/
relationships/ismarriagedivorcerev1.shtml

JUDAISM:
www.bbc.co.uk/schools/gcsebitesize/rs/
relationships/jumarriagedivorcerev1.shtml

SIKHISM:
www.bbc.co.uk/schools/gcsebitesize/rs/
relationships/simarriageanddivorcerev1.shtml

GLOSSARY

affectionate	showing love, usually by physical things such as kissing or hugging
aisle	a walkway between rows of seats
committed	when something has been promised or someone has pledged to do something
court	a place where legal decisions can be made
credit card	a plastic card given out by banks which allow people to buy things and pay for it later
documents	pieces of information which can be written down or stored electronically
founder	the person that starts or establishes something, like a religion
gender inequality	where men and women are not treated equally
honour	a quality where someone or something is known to keep promises, act honestly and do what is right
international	something that involves more than one country
matchmaker	a person who puts two people together in a romantic relationship
Middle Ages	a period in European history between A.D. 500 and A.D. 1500
official	relating to an authority
old-fashioned	not modern
opportunities	chances to do something, often positive
possessions	objects that belong to someone
property	an object which is owned; usually a building or piece of land
protests	actions that express a disapproval of, or objection to something, usually involving multiple people
recited	read out from memory
registrar	a person who looks after official records
relationships	the connections between people
represents	stands for, or is a symbol of something
rights	things that everyone deserves to have or be able to do
sacred	connected to a god or gods
sapling	young tree
sex	either male or female
society	a collection of people living together
traditions	beliefs or behaviours that have been passed down from one generation to the next
valued	important or worth something to someone
violent	using force to physically hurt someone

INDEX